ESSENTIAL ELEMENTS
FOR JAZZ ENSEMBLE
Book 2

A COMPREHENSIVE METHOD FOR JAZZ STYLE AND IMPROVISATION

By MIKE STEINEL

Managing Editor:
MICHAEL SWEENEY

THREE BASIC SECTIONS

I. **Daily Drills, Warm-ups, and Workouts**

II. **Improvisation Lessons**

III. **Performance Spotlights (Repertoire)**

This book is the second in a series and is designed for developing musicians and ensembles. The first book: *Essential Elements for Jazz Ensemble* is a comprehensive introduction to the jazz style, theory, improvisation and history. The exercises and compositions in this book can be played by a full jazz ensemble, combo, or individually with the recordings. The nine compositions for full band cover a variety of styles, tempos, and keys, and include Demonstration Solos for study and reference.

The recordings are available as a free download. Visit www.halleonard.com/mylibrary and use the code printed below to access your mp3s.

We hope you find this book helpful, and always remember…have fun playing jazz.

PLAYBACK+
Speed • Pitch • Balance • Loop

To access audio visit:
www.halleonard.com/mylibrary

Enter Code
J2DM-3604-5923-2949

ISBN 978-1-4950-7912-2

HAL•LEONARD®
7777 W. BLUEMOUND RD. P.O. BOX 13819 MILWAUKEE, WI 53213

THE BASICS OF JAZZ DRUMS
Review from *Essential Elements for Jazz Ensemble* (Book 1)
NOTE: Some drum notation has evolved since the publication of Book 1.

The Drum Set
Jazz drummers use a drum set that generally contains the following parts:
- Ride Cymbal
- Hi-Hat or Sock Cymbal
- Tom Tom(s)
- Crash Cymbal
- Snare Drum
- Bass Drum w/foot pedal

The Set-Up
The Drum Set should be set up so all the instruments can be reached comfortably. This will be different for each individual drummer. Here is an example of a typical set-up.

Reading a Drum Part
Drum set reading is different than other instruments. It is written on a five-line staff using a special clef sign or none at all. Notes with regular noteheads indicate drums (snare, bass, and toms) and notes with special "X" noteheads indicate cymbals. The hi-hat and bass drum will be played by the feet unless otherwise notated. Each instrument is assigned a particular lines as follows:

Other Special Notation

Drum Rolls

Cymbal Rolls

The Special Hi-Hat Notation

Open Hi-Hat

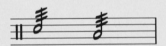

Indicated by "H.H." and a circle over the note. Played with hi-hat partially open.

Closed Hi-Hat

Indicated by "H.H." and a plus sign over the note. Played with hi-hat closed.

Common Hi-Hat Swing Pattern

Sounds like: Cheer Chick Cha Cheer Chick Cha

Note:
"Open" or "Closed" may appear only when a change occurs.

Foot Technique in Jazz Drumming

The Bass Drum
There are two basic techniques: (1) the heel remains on the heel plate and the pedal is played with ankle motion and (2) the heel is elevated and the pedal is played with the ball of the foot. Experiment with each to find which is best for you.

The Hi-Hat
There are various techniques to playing the hi-hat but it is suggested that students begin with the "rocking" or "heel-toe" technique. In this method the foot rocks by bending at the ankle. The heel comes down on the heel plate on beats 1 and 3, and the ball of the foot comes down on the pedal on beats 2 and 4. This produces a crisp hi-hat "chick" on beats 2 and 4 and is a fundamental part of playing the basic swing pattern.

The Ride Cymbal

In jazz marked "swing" the ride cymbal reinforces the quarter note walking bass line provided by the bass player. These two instruments supply the rhythmic foundation of swing music.

The Basic Ride Cymbal Pattern

The ride cymbal pattern is usually played in a triplet feel, however it is not always strict. At slow tempos the pattern is very triplety but at faster tempos the eighth notes are played more evenly. In this book we will always notate the ride pattern in eighth notes.

The basic Ride Cymbal Pattern is notated as: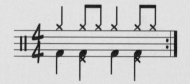

The basic Ride Cymbal Pattern sounds like: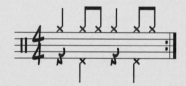

The Basic Swing Pattern – Playing "time"

This is the basic swing pattern for Jazz Drumming (with and without bass drum). Practice each until they are "automatic".

Achieving Variety of the Ride Pattern

Although many drum parts are notated with a strictly repetitive ride cymbal pattern, in practice jazz drummers use a wide variety of cymbal rhythms. Practice each of the rhythms below so that you can execute them with steady time and good feel. When playing the exercises and songs in this book feel free to use any of the rhythmic patterns listed below.

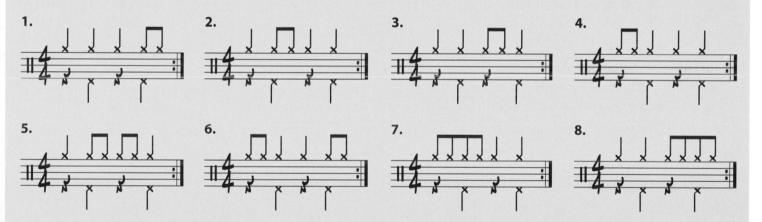

Using the Bass Drum in the Swing Pattern

When playing the basic swing pattern the bass drum can play quarter notes on all four beats of the bar very softly or it can be omitted. It is important to develop a very light bass drum as it can easily sound heavy and cover up the notes of the bass line. It is often said that the bass drum should be "felt but not heard"..

Playing with the Ensemble (Playing "Figures")

In jazz the drummer does more than just play the beat pattern of the song (often called "playing time"). Good jazz drummers usually adjust their playing to fit the melodies and rhythms that the ensemble plays. These melodies and rhythms are called "figures."

There are two basic types of figures:
  1. Ensemble "figures" played by the entire band
  2. Section "figures" played by one section

Figures may be interpreted in a variety of ways. Ensemble figures can be reinforced with snare, bass drum, toms, and cymbals, while section figures are most often reinforced lightly while the ride cymbal and hi-hat continue to play the basic beat pattern of the music. It is important that the drum part enhance and not detract from the overall effect of the music.

What Do Figures Look Like?

Composers differ in how they notate ensemble and section "figures."

The band plays:

The drum part looks like: — Slashes in the staff with small (cues) notes indicating the rhythm of the ensemble.

Or this: — The basic rhythm notated in slashes in the staff.

Or this: — The basic rhythm notated in drum notation.

How Are Figures Played (Interpreted)?

Figures such as the ones above can be played a number of ways. When learning a song it is best to play simple reinforcing rhythms in the snare drum. As you learn the "figures" better you can use more complicated rhythms and incorporate the toms, bass drum, and cymbals.

The drum part looks like:

Can be played simply: — The basic rhythm is played by the snare while the ride cymbal and hi-hat play "time". This works good for "section" figures

Can be more complex: — The basic rhythm is reinforced and enhanced by snare, toms, bass drum and crash cymbal. This works well for figures that are played by the entire band.

Note: *This is only a suggested interpretation.*

Figures Versus Swinging

It is important that drummers never let the playing of figures disturb the time and feel of the music.

Playing Drum Fills

Drum Fills are short improvised drum solos that are:
1. used to "fill in" space after ensemble figures
2. used to "set-up" or prepare the listener for ensemble figures
3. used to mark off the main sections in a piece of music
4. used as solo breaks in a jazz arrangement

What Should You Play?

Drum Fills can be very simple or very complex. They can involve as few as one drum (good "swinging" rhythms on the snare drum can work well) or as many as all the drums and cymbals of your drum set. It is important that the fill you choose fit the style of the music and not disturb the tempo or the logical "flow" of the arrangement you are playing.

Here is an example of some simple fills used to "set-up" an ensemble figure and then "fill-in" or lead-in to the next section of the arrangement:

The drum part looks like:

Can be played simply:

Can be more complex:

THE BASICS OF JAZZ STYLE
Review from *Essential Elements for Jazz Ensemble* (Book 1)

Jazz Articulation Review

These are the four basic articulations in jazz and the related scat syllables for each. "Doo", "Bah", "Dit" and "Dot" can be used to remind us (aurally) of the sound. However, these are not necessarily how we will articulate on the individual instruments.

| **Tenuto** (full value) | **Staccato** (short, unaccented) | **Long Accent** (full value, accented) | **Roof Top Accent** (short, accented) |
| Doo | Dit | Bah | Dot |

Attacks and Releases

In traditional music you use a "Tah" articulation to begin a note and taper the note at the end.

In jazz it is common to use a "Doo" attack (soft and legato) to begin a note. It is also common to end the note with the tongue. This "tongue-stop" gives the music a rhythmic feeling.

Accenting "2 and 4"

For most traditional music the important beats in 4/4 time are 1 and 3. In jazz, however, the emphasis is usually on beats 2 and 4. Emphasizing "2 and 4" gives the music a jazz feeling.

Quarter Notes

In swing style quarter notes are usually played detached. In Latin or Rock they may be played with a variety of articulations but are often played full value.

Swing 8th Notes Sound Different Than They Look

In swing the 2nd 8th note of each beat is actually played like the last third of a triplet, and slightly accented. 8th notes in swing style are usually played legato.

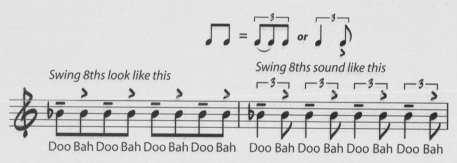

8ths in Latin and Rock (Straight 8th Music)

8th Notes in Latin or Rock are played evenly and the articulations are often quite different than in swing style.

This page intentionally left blank

DAILY DRILLS, WARM-UPS AND WORKOUTS

1. BASIC SCALE AND STYLE WORKOUT #1 – Major Scale

2. BASIC SCALE AND STYLE WORKOUT #2 – Major Scale

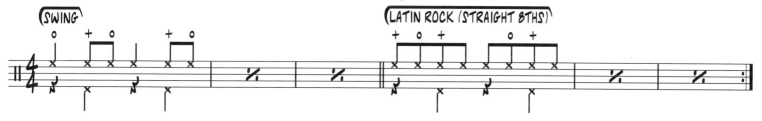

3. BASIC SCALE AND STYLE WORKOUT #3 – Mixolydian Mode

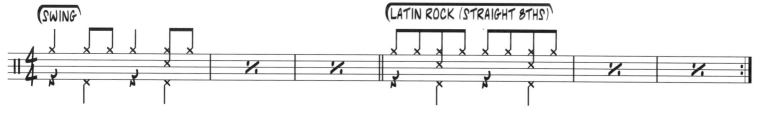

4. BASIC SCALE AND STYLE WORKOUT #4 – Mixolydian Mode

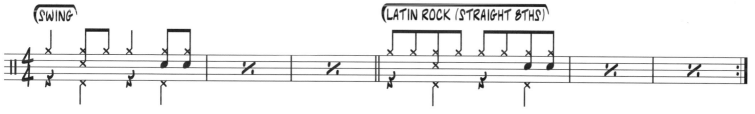

5. BASIC SCALE AND STYLE WORKOUT #5 – Dorian Mode

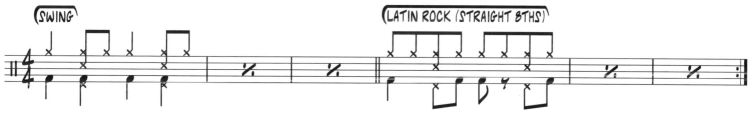

6. BASIC SCALE AND STYLE WORKOUT #6 – Harmonic Minor

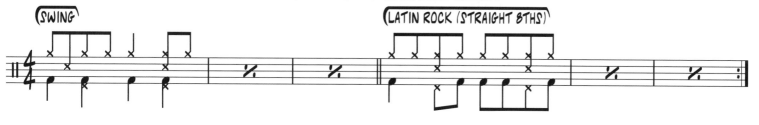

RHYTHM WORKOUTS FOR READING AND STYLE

All exercises are played in a Swing style. Play the Hi-Hat on beats 2 and 4 for the exercises on this page.

7. HALF MEASURE RHYTHMS

8. COMBINING COMMON RHYTHMS #1

9. COMBINING COMMON RHYTHMS #2

10. COMBINING COMMON RHYTHMS #3

11. COMBINING COMMON RHYTHMS #4

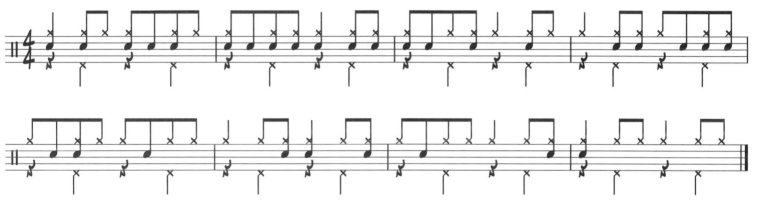

12. COMBINING COMMON RHYTHMS #5

13. COMBINING COMMON RHYTHMS #6 – Adding Ties

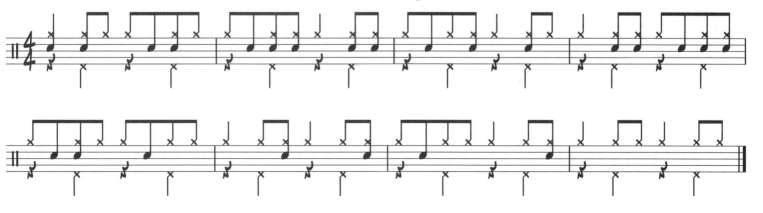

RHYTHM WORKOUTS FOR READING AND STYLE (STRAIGHT 8THS)

14. COMBINING COMMON RHYTHMS #7

15. COMBINING COMMON RHYTHMS #8

16. SCALE AND RHYTHM WORKOUT

17. MELODY AND RHYTHM WORKOUT #1

18. MELODY AND RHYTHM WORKOUT #2

JAZZ EXPRESSION WORKOUTS

All exercises are played in a Swing style. Play a basic swing pattern while reinforcing horn rhythms (cued above staff).

19. STYLE CONCEPT – Syllables for Jazz Expression

20. SCOOPS, FALLS, BENDS AND DOITS

21. PLOPS, GLISSANDI AND FLIPS

22. MELODY AND EXPRESSION WORKOUT #1

23. MELODY AND RHYTHM WORKOUT #2

24. NEW CONCEPT: GHOSTED NOTES

Often single notes in jazz lines are played very softly and without accent. Lines with ghosted 8th notes are usually played legato.

25. JAZZ EXPRESSION ETUDE

Playing With Brushes

Brushes are used to produce a smooth pulse at softer volumes. There many different approaches to brush playing. Often in Latin and country music brushes are used as if they are regular drumsticks. In jazz performed at slow and medium tempos brush playing uses the same technique and grip as stick playing with one difference: at least one of the brushes (usually the left) maintains direct contact with the drum head at all times. The diagrams below shows a basic brush pattern in 4/4 swing time and a common variation.

Basic Brush Pattern in 4/4 Swing

The Right Brush plays the basic swing cymbal pattern by tapping back and forth
The brush is lifted between beats.

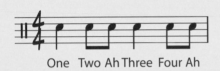

The Left Brush makes a clockwise circle on the drumhead every two beats. If consistent contact is maintained the sound will be a steady "swish" and the hands will seem to cross on beats 2 and 4. For slower tempos each circle can last one beat.

Variation:

Both hands move in opposite directions in a circular motion (one hand clockwise and the other counter-clockwise). To get the "feel" for this technique, practice making circles in time with both hands producing a steady "swishing" sound.

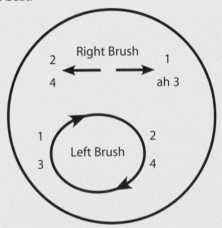

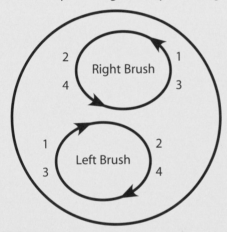

Hints:
- Accents can be achieved by lifting the brush and tapping the drum head or by sweeping with a bit more weight.
- Some techniques combine the "swishing" sweep with a lifting and tapping motion in one of the hands.
- Generally only the tip of the brush is used for softer volumes. For louder volumes or more aggressive accents two or three inches of the brush can strike the drum head.

Playing the brushes in 3/4 time requires that the beat pattern (in the "tapping" hand) be adjusted to:

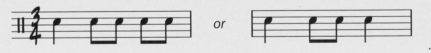

WARM-UPS FOR BALANCE BLEND AND INTONATION

All exercises are played in a Swing style.

26. BALANCE AND BLEND WORKOUT (Concert B♭ Major)

27. BALANCE AND BLEND WORKOUT (Concert F Major)

28. BALANCE AND BLEND WORKOUT (Concert B♭ Mixolydian)

29. BALANCE AND BLEND WORKOUT (Concert F Mixolydian)

30. BALANCE AND BLEND WORKOUT (Concert E♭ Mixolydian)

31. BALANCE AND BLEND WORKOUT (Concert C Mixolydian)

32. BALANCE AND BLEND WORKOUT (Concert C Dorian)

MAJOR SCALES BY NUMBERS

33. MAJOR SCALE WORKOUT

34. MAJOR SCALE BY THE NUMBERS #1

35. MAJOR SCALE BY THE NUMBERS #2

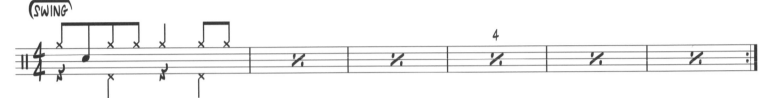

36. MAJOR SCALE BY THE NUMBERS #3

37. MAJOR SCALE BY THE NUMBERS #4

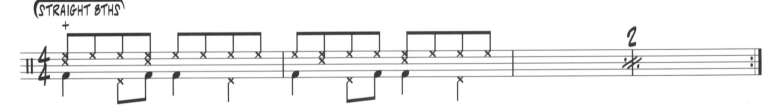

38. MAJOR SCALE BY THE NUMBERS #5

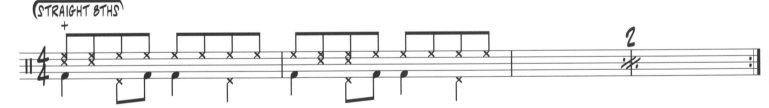

39. MAJOR SCALE BY THE NUMBERS #6

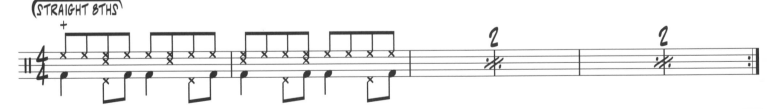

Additional Workouts – Repeat the scale patterns in exercises 34 through 39 using these common keys.

MIXOLYDIAN MODE BY NUMBERS

40. MIXOLYDIAN WORKOUT

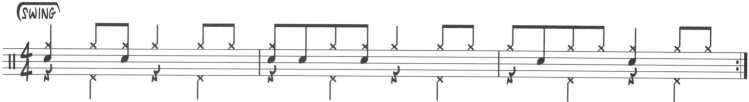

41. MIXOLYDIAN BY THE NUMBERS #1

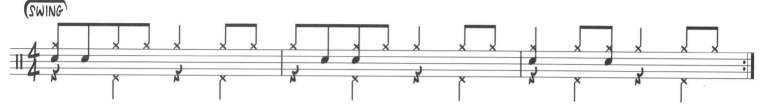

42. MIXOLYDIAN BY THE NUMBERS #2

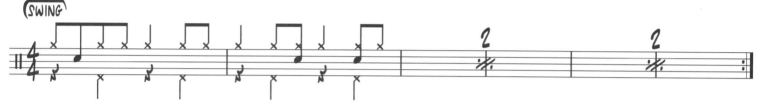

43. MIXOLYDIAN BY THE NUMBERS #3

44. MIXOLYDIAN BY THE NUMBERS #4

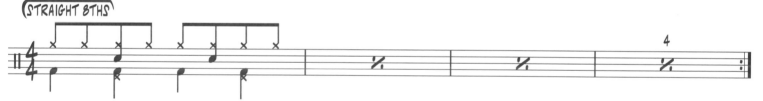

45. MIXOLYDIAN BY THE NUMBERS #5

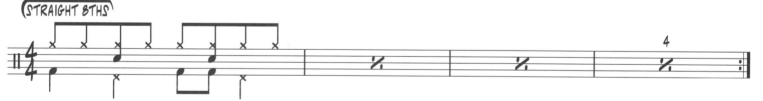

46. MIXOLYDIAN BY THE NUMBERS #6

Additional Workouts – Repeat the scale patterns in exercises 40 through 46 using these common Mixolydian modes.

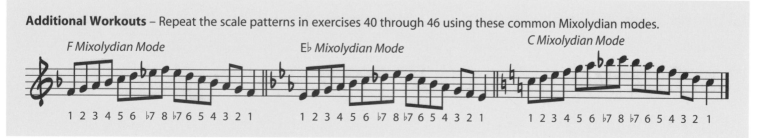

DORIAN MODE BY NUMBERS

47. DORIAN WORKOUT

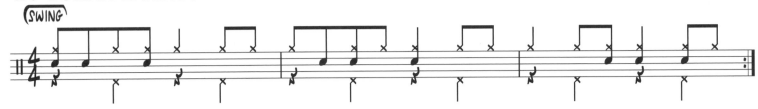

48. DORIAN BY THE NUMBERS #1

49. DORIAN BY THE NUMBERS #2

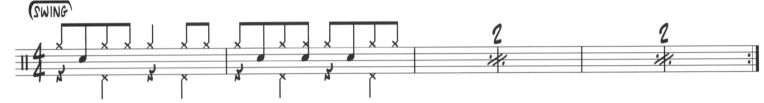

50. DORIAN BY THE NUMBERS #3

51. DORIAN BY THE NUMBERS #4

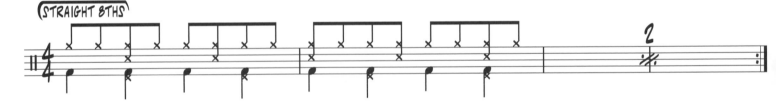

52. DORIAN BY THE NUMBERS #5

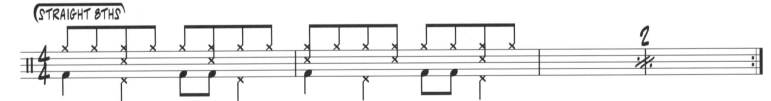

53. DORIAN BY THE NUMBERS #6

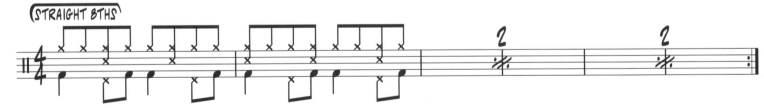

Additional Workouts – Repeat the scale patterns in exercises 47 through 53 using these common Dorian modes.

SCALE WORKOUTS – PENTATONIC AND BLUES SCALES IN CONCERT B♭

54. SCALE WORKOUT #1 – Minor Pentatonic

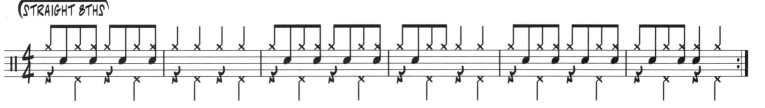

55. SCALE WORKOUT #2 – Minor Pentatonic

56. SCALE WORKOUT #3 – Minor Blues

57. SCALE WORKOUT #4 – Minor Blues

58. SCALE WORKOUT #5 – Major Blues

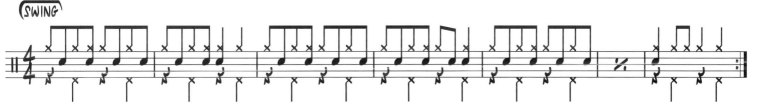

59. SCALE WORKOUT #6 – Major Blues

SCALE WORKOUTS – PENTATONIC AND BLUES SCALES IN CONCERT F

60. SCALE WORKOUT #1 – Minor Pentatonic

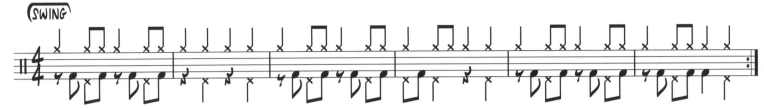

61. SCALE WORKOUT #2 – Minor Pentatonic

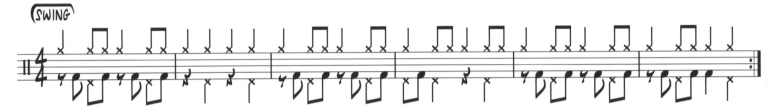

62. SCALE WORKOUT #3 – Minor Blues

63. SCALE WORKOUT #4 – Minor Blues

64. SCALE WORKOUT #5 – Major Blues

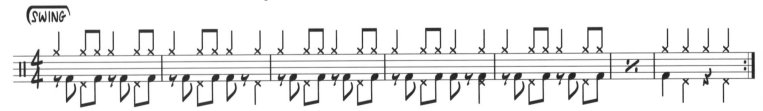

65. SCALE WORKOUT #6 – Major Blues

ADVANCED WORKOUTS – PENTATONIC AND BLUES SCALES IN CONCERT B♭

66. ADVANCED WORKOUT #1 – Minor Pentatonic

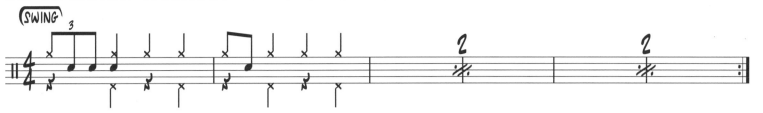

67. ADVANCED WORKOUT #2 – Minor Pentatonic

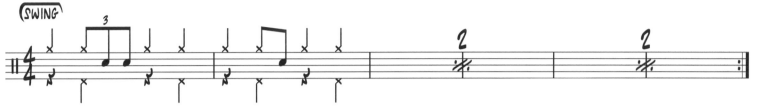

68. ADVANCED WORKOUT #3 – Minor Blues

69. ADVANCED WORKOUT #4 – Major Blues

70. ADVANCED WORKOUT #5 – Blues Riffs

71. ADVANCED WORKOUT #6 – Blues Riffs

ADVANCED WORKOUTS – PENTATONIC AND BLUES SCALES IN CONCERT F

72. ADVANCED WORKOUT #1 – Minor Pentatonic

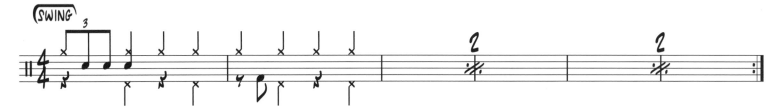

73. ADVANCED WORKOUT #2 – Minor Pentatonic

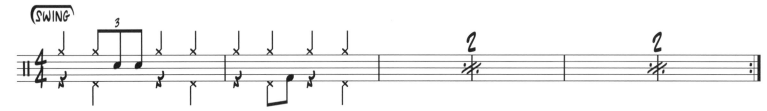

74. ADVANCED WORKOUT #3 – Minor Blues

75. ADVANCED WORKOUT #4 – Major Blues

76. ADVANCED WORKOUT #5 – Blues Riffs

77. ADVANCED WORKOUT #6 – Blues Riffs

LESSON #1 *Reinventing Melody*

Improvisation Concept – *Improvising by changing the rhythms of a melody (Reinvention).*

All Lesson #1 exercises are played in a Swing style.

78. SIMPLE MELODY *Start with a simple familiar melody.*

79. SYNCOPATION *Play notes early or late.*

80. ITERATION *Fill up long notes with rhythm.*

81. DISPLACEMENT *Move melody around.*

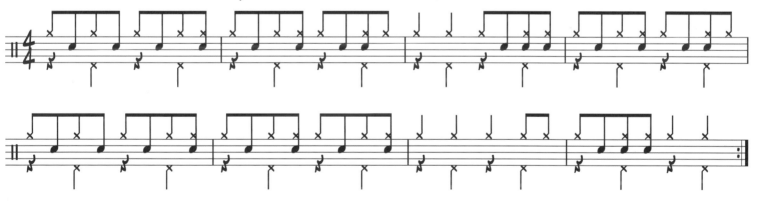

82. AUGMENTATION AND DIMINUTION *Make notes longer or shorter.*

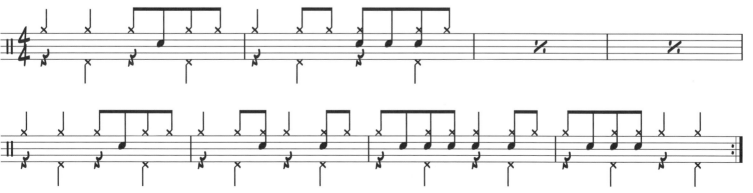

83. REPETITION AND TRUNCATION *Repeat notes or leave them out.*

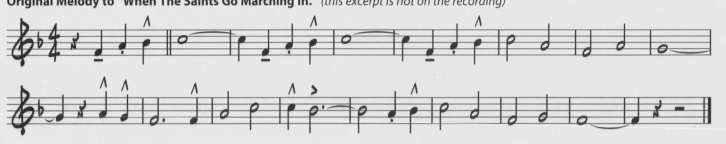

Original Melody to "When The Saints Go Marching In." *(this excerpt is not on the recording)*

84. SAINTS REINVENTED *Compare this reinvented version with the original melody.*

LESSON #2 *Ornamenting Melody*

Improvisation Concept – *Improvising by adding notes to a melody (Ornamentation).*

All Lesson #2 exercises are played with Straight 8ths.

85. SIMPLE SHOO FLY *Start with a simple familiar melody.*

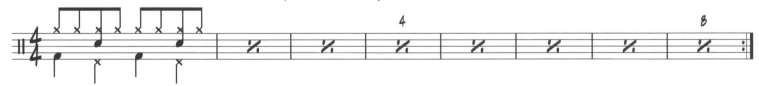

86. NEIGHBOR TONES *Add notes below or above the melody.*

87. PASSING TONES *Add notes between the melody notes.*

88. ENCLOSING TONES *Add notes above and below the melody. Usually a step or half step above and a half step below.*

89. CHROMATIC APPROACH TONES *Add notes a half step away from the melody.*

90. DOUBLE CHROMATIC APPROACH TONES *Add two chromatic notes to a melody.*

91. ORNAMENTING SAINTS *"When The Saints Go Marching In" with ornaments.*

23

...nerally recognized as the birthplace of jazz, was a major economic and cultural center in the southern United ...nning of the 20th century. The very first jazz ensembles were the brass bands that played in a ragtime style. ...s from New Orleans include:

Buddy Bolden	Sidney Bechet	Fats Domino	Dr. John
Louis Armstrong	Wynton Marsalis	Professor Longhair	The Dirty Dozen Brass Band
Jelly Roll Morton	Harry Connick Jr.	Louis Prima	Terence Blanchard

Rhythmic Concept – *"Second Line Rhythmic Feel"* is a style of drumming that originated in New Orleans. The 8th notes in a *"Second Line"* feel are played between what would be straight 8ths and regular triplet-oriented swing 8th notes.

92. STRAIGHT, SWING AND SECOND LINE 8TH NOTES

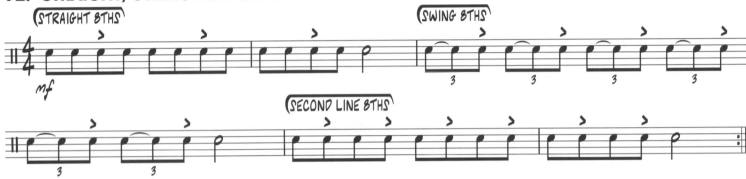

Rhythmic Concept – *Tresillo Rhythm* is a three note rhythm which is very common in New Orleans music and early Rock 'n' Roll.

93. WORKOUT FOR RHYTHMIC FEEL AND GROOVE

94. MELODY WORKOUT FOR "SAINTS"

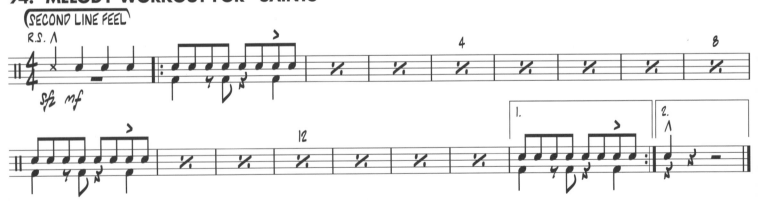

95. MELODY WORKOUT FOR "SWING LOW"

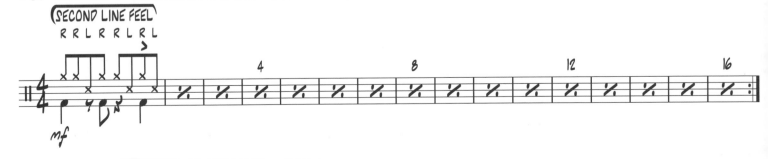

96. THE SAINTS ARE SWINGIN' LOW – Full Band Arrangement

97. DEMONSTRATION SOLO FOR "THE SAINTS ARE SWINGIN' LOW"

98. PRACTICE TRACK FOR "THE SAINTS ARE SWINGIN' LOW" – mm. 26-42 (3 choruses)

LESSON #3 *Blues Riffs*

Improvisation Concept – *Riffs are short melodies that are common parts of jazz solos often using notes of the blues scales (minor and major). Blues songs and solos often use three identical four-bar riffs.*

All Lesson #3 exercises are played in a Swing style.
For each exercise in this lesson the bass drum should be played very lightly ("feathered").

99. BLUES RIFF #1 *Blues Riff played 3 times over a twelve-bar blues.*

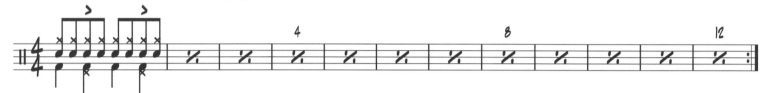

100. BLUES RIFF #2

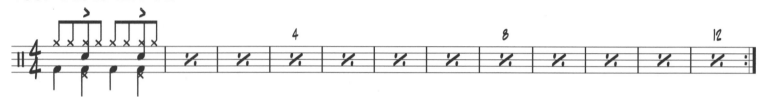

101. "ROVING THIRD" RIFF #1

102. "ROVING THIRD" RIFF #2

103. "ROVING THIRD" RIFF #3

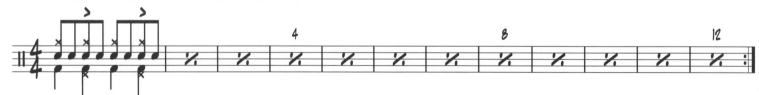

104. "ROVING THIRD" RIFF #4

LESSON #4 *Call and Response*

Improvisation Concept – *Call and Response* is a traditional way of playing or singing melodies common in African American Church music of the 19th and 20th centuries.

All Lesson #4 exercises are played in a Swing style.

105. CALL AND RESPONSE #1

106. CALL AND RESPONSE #2

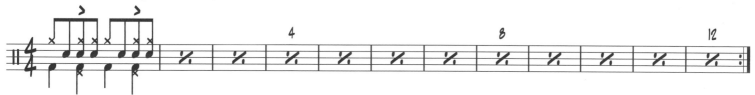

107. CALL AND RESPONSE #3

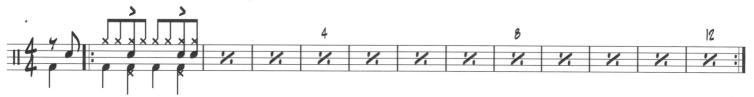

Improvisation Concept – *Improvising using Short Call and Response Riffs. Often songs and solos use two-bar phrases in a "Call and Response" style. The responses usually start in bars 3, 7, and 11 and are similar or identical.*

108. CALL AND RESPONSE #4   *Play 3 Times – Listen, play, then improvise by changing the rhythm.*

109. CALL AND RESPONSE #5   *Play 3 Times – Listen, play, then improvise by changing the rhythm.*

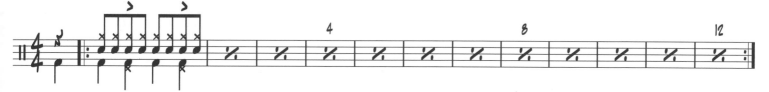

PERFORMANCE SPOTLIGHT *Vine Street Ruckus*

In the 1930s **Kansas City** was home to some of the greatest musicians in jazz. Bands led by Count Basie and Jay McShann played a swing style of music that drew heavily on the blues tradition of "Call and Response." Important musicians from or associated with Kansas City Jazz:

Charlie Parker	Claude Williams	Buck Clayton	Hot Lips Page	Count Basie
Bobby Watson	Coleman Hawkins	Lester Young	Jay McShann	Pat Metheny
Bob Brookmeyer	Ben Webster	Andy Kirk	Mary Lou Williams	Jimmy Rushing
Walter Page	Jimmy Lunceford	Hershel Evans	Big Joe Turner	Bennie Moten

110. MELODY WORKOUT #1 – Main Riff

111. MELODY WORKOUT #2 – Response Riff

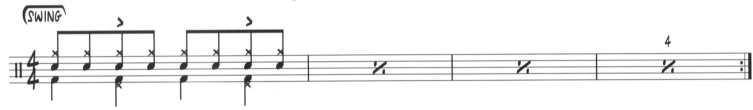

112. "VINE STREET RUCKUS" – Full Band Arrangement

113. DEMONSTRATION SOLO FOR "VINE STREET RUCKUS"

114. PRACTICE TRACK FOR "VINE STREET RUCKUS" – mm. 45-56 (4 choruses)

LESSON #5 Mixolydian Vamp and Chromatic Passing Tones

Theory Concept – *Many jazz songs are written using the Mixolydian Mode. Interesting vamps can be made by building a chord on each note of the mode. A **"Vamp"** is a repeated musical pattern.*

All Lesson #5 exercises are played with Straight 8ths.

115. MIXOLYDIAN WORKOUT #1

116. MIXOLYDIAN WORKOUT #2

117. IMPROVISING ON MODAL VAMPS

Improvisation Concept – *Chromatic Passing Tones can be added to a mode between the whole steps.*

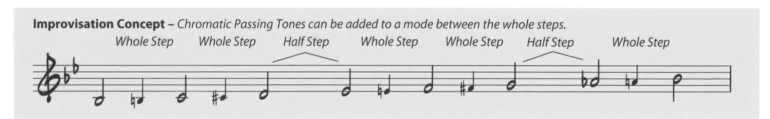

118. ADDING CHROMATIC NOTES

119. PASSING TONE WORKOUT #1

120. PASSING TONE WORKOUT #2

121. PASSING TONE WORKOUT #3

LESSON #6 *Composite Blues Scale*

Theory Concept – *The Composite Blues Scale* is formed by combining the Minor Blues Scale and the Major Blues Scale. The Composite Blues Scale has 9 different notes.

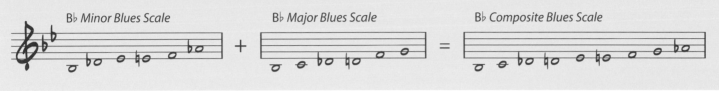

All Lesson #6 exercises are played with Straight 8ths.

122. THEORY WORKOUT   *Compare the Minor, Major, and Composite Blues Scales.*

123. COMPOSITE BLUES SCALE WORKOUT #1

124. COMPOSITE BLUES SCALE WORKOUT #2

125. COMPOSITE BLUES SCALE WORKOUT #3

PERFORMANCE SPOTLIGHT *Beale Street Barbeque*

On December 15, 1977, **Beale Street** (in Memphis, TN) was officially declared the "Home of the Blues" by an act of the U.S. Congress. Memphis was an important music center throughout the 20th century and Memphis musicians influenced all types of American music including jazz, blues, soul, gospel and Rock 'n' Roll. Famous musicians associated with Memphis include:

Elvis Presley	Howlin' Wolf	Booker T. Jones	Memphis Minnie	W.C. Handy
Aretha Franklin	B.B. King	Isaac Hayes	Booker Little	George Coleman

126. MELODY WORKOUT

127. RHYTHM WORKOUT – Bass Vamp

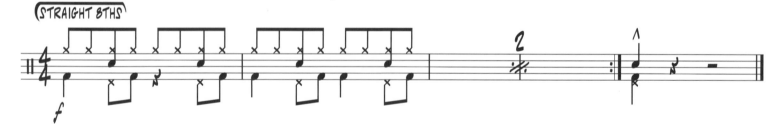

128. "BEALE STREET BARBEQUE" – Full Band Arrangement

129. DEMONSTRATION SOLO FOR "BEALE STREET BARBEQUE"

130. PRACTICE TRACK FOR "BEALE STREET BARBEQUE" – mm. 35-42 (6 choruses)

LESSON #7 *Triplets in Swing and Dorian Vamp*

Improvisation Concept – *Triplets are very important in making jazz swing. Often the underlying rhythmic subdivision in swing is the triplet. Not all music in a swing feel is interpreted as a strict triplet. Generally at faster tempos the 8ths are more equal in value.*

All Lesson #7 exercises are played in a Swing style.

131. TRIPLET WORKOUT #1

132. TRIPLET WORKOUT #2

133. TRIPLET WORKOUT #3

Theory Review – The Major Scale has seven modes. *Each mode is built on a different note of the scale. Each mode has a unique sound, unique name, and works well with a specific chord type. Ionian is another name for the Major Scale.*

134. SEVEN MODES OF THE MAJOR SCALE (Concert B♭)

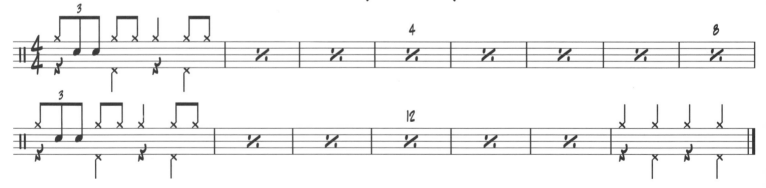

135. DORIAN WORKOUT *Play the mode then pick any note in the chords.*

LESSON #8 *Dorian Vamp and Minor Pentatonic Scale*

136. DORIAN VAMP

137. DORIAN WORKOUT WITH TRIPLETS

The recorded grooves for exercises 137–140 are the same. If not using the recording, use the written exercises to experiment with different grooves.

138. DORIAN MODE – 9th, 6th, and 11th

139. DORIAN/MINOR PENTATONIC

140. MINOR PENTATONIC WORKOUT WITH TRIPLETS

PERFORMANCE SPOTLIGHT *Windy City*

Musicians from New Orleans such as Joe "King" Oliver and Louis Armstrong brought jazz to **Chicago** in the 1920s and became important influences for the local musicians. The "Windy City" quickly became an important center for jazz music and remains so today. Some important musicians from Chicago include:

Paul Butterfield	Nat King Cole	Jack DeJohnette	Kurt Elling	Chaka Khan	Benny Goodman
Lester Bowie	Bud Freeman	Dinah Washington	Herbie Hancock	Gene Krupa	Ramsey Lewis
Chicago (The Band)	Lou Rawls	Lennie Tristano	Jimmy McPartland	Lil Hardin Armstrong	Buddy Guy

141. RHYTHM WORKOUT

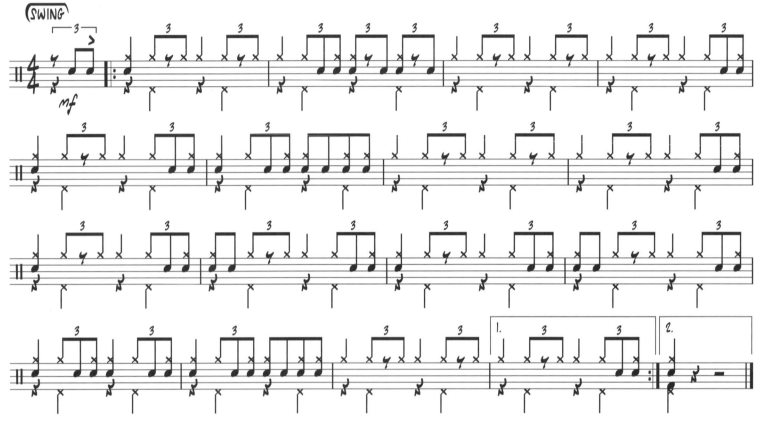

142. MELODY WORKOUT

143. COUNTER MELODY WORKOUT

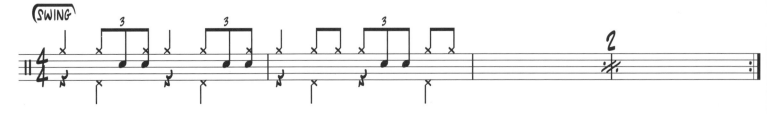

144. "WINDY CITY" – Full Band Arrangement

145. DEMONSTRATION SOLO FOR "WINDY CITY"

146. PRACTICE TRACK FOR "WINDY CITY" – mm. 26-33 (4 choruses)

LESSON #9 Bebop Scale and Double-Time Playing

All Lesson #9 exercises are played with Straight 8ths.

147. MIXOLYDIAN MODE/BEBOP SCALE

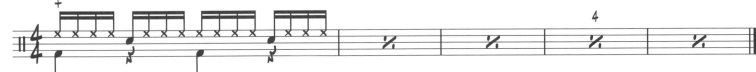

148. MIXOLYDIAN MODE/BEBOP SCALE WORKOUT

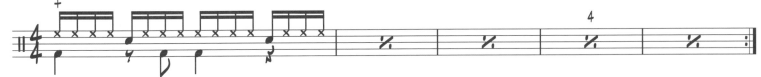

149. BEBOP LICK WORKOUT #1

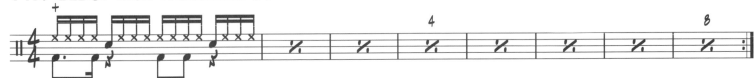

150. BEBOP LICK WORKOUT #2

151. BEBOP LICK WORKOUT #3

Rhythmic Concept – *Double Time* (or ***"Doubling Up"***) *is often played with 16th note rhythms. These will sound the same as 8th note rhythms at a faster tempo but with a "half time feel."*

152. DOUBLE-TIME WORKOUT #1

153. DOUBLE-TIME WORKOUT #2

154. DOUBLE-TIME WORKOUT #3

LESSON #10 *The Ten-Note Bebop Scale*

All Lesson #10 exercises are played with Straight 8ths.

155. TEN-NOTE MIXOLYDIAN BEBOP SCALE

156. TEN-NOTE MIXOLYDIAN BEBOP SCALE WORKOUT #1

157. TEN-NOTE MIXOLYDIAN BEBOP SCALE WORKOUT #2

158. ADDING CHROMATIC NOTES

PERFORMANCE SPOTLIGHT *Baytown Boogaloo*

Tower Of Power has been one of the most successful jazz/rock fusion ensembles since the 1970s. Formed in Oakland, CA, their sound is a unique blend of Rhythm & Blues elements, precision horn section work, tightly constructed bass lines, and infectious drum grooves. Much of their music is played in a 16th note rock feel. "Baytown Boogaloo" is written in a *Tower of Power* style.

159. 16TH NOTE WORKOUT

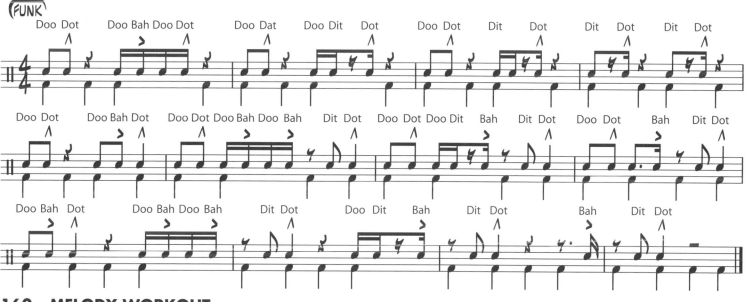

160. MELODY WORKOUT

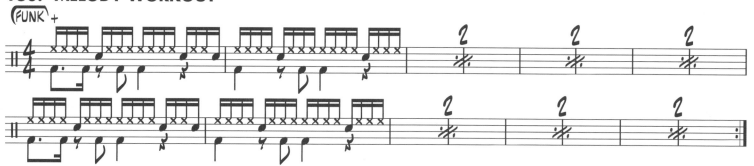

40

161. "BAYTOWN BOOGALOO" – Full Band Arrangement

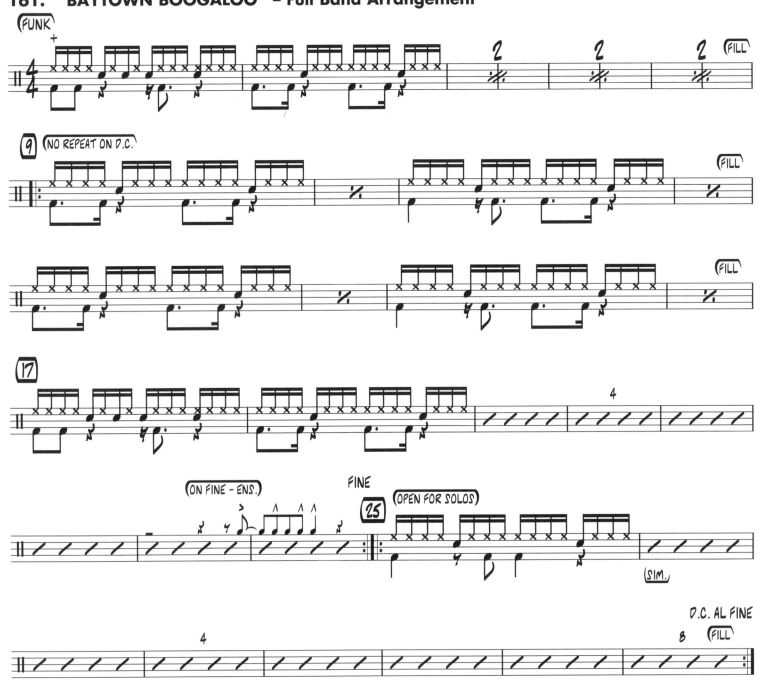

162. DEMONSTRATION SOLO FOR "BAYTOWN BOOGALOO"

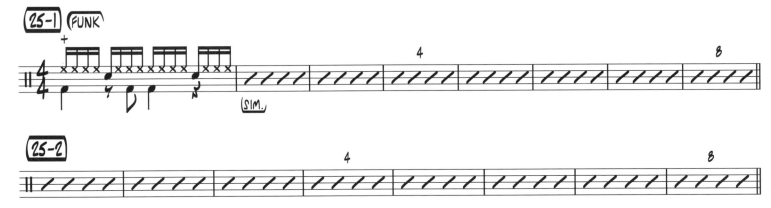

163. PRACTICE TRACK FOR "BAYTOWN BOOGALOO" – mm. 25-32 (4 choruses)

LESSON #11 *9th Chords and Chord Tone Soloing*

All Lesson #11 exercises are played in a Swing style.

164. DOMINANT 7TH AND 9TH CHORDS

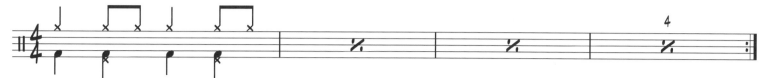

165. TYPICAL PROGRESSION USING DOMINANT 9TH CHORD

166. CHORD TONE WORKOUT

Rhythmic Concept – *For rhythmic variety add Triplets and start on upbeats.*

167. TRIPLET ARPEGGIOS

168. ARPEGGIOS STARTING ON 3

169. ARPEGGIOS STARTING ON 9

170. ARPEGGIOS STARTING ON 5

LESSON #12 *Chromatic and Passing Tones*

All Lesson #12 exercises are played in a Swing style. The recorded grooves for exercises 171–178 are the same. If not using the recording, use the written exercises to experiment with different grooves.

171. CHROMATIC TONE BELOW THE ROOT

172. CHROMATIC TONE BELOW THE THIRD

173. STARTING ON THE UPBEAT AND ADDING A TRIPLET

174. CHROMATIC TONE BELOW THE FIFTH

175. CHROMATIC TONE BELOW THE NINTH

176. ADDING 2 BETWEEN 1 AND 3

177. ADDING 6 BETWEEN 5 AND 7

178. PASSING TONE WORKOUT

PERFORMANCE SPOTLIGHT *Liberty Bell Shuffle*

The Declaration of Independence was ratified in **Philadelphia** on July 4, 1776. Important jazz musicians from Philadelphia include:

John Coltrane	Philly Joe Jones	Michael Brecker	Randy Brecker	Clifford Brown	Stan Getz
Billie Holiday	Jimmy McGriff	Lee Morgan	McCoy Tyner	Stanley Clarke	Kenny Barron
Pat Martino	Bobby Timmons	Red Rodney	Jimmy Garrison	Sonny Fortune	Hank Mobley
Jimmy Smith	Archie Shepp	Rashied Ali			

179. MELODY WORKOUT

180. "LIBERTY BELL SHUFFLE" – Full Band Arrangement

Bah Doo Bah— Bah Doo Bah   Bah Doo Dot

44

181. DEMONSTRATION SOLO FOR "LIBERTY BELL SHUFFLE"

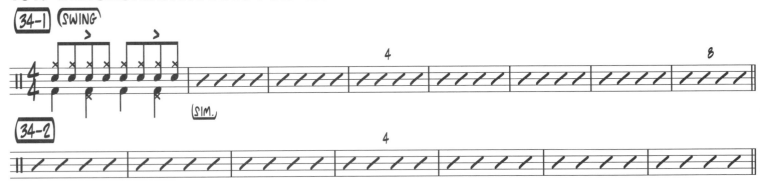

182. PRACTICE TRACK FOR "LIBERTY BELL SHUFFLE" – mm. 34-41 (4 choruses)

LESSON #13 *ii–V–I in Major and Minor*

Theory Concept – *Chord Function in Major and Minor*. *A chord can be built on each step of the major and minor scales. The chords are often labeled using Roman Numerals.*

All Lesson #13 exercises are played with Straight 8ths.

183. CHORDS OF MAJOR AND RELATIVE MINOR KEYS
Relative Minor has the same notes and key signature as Major but starts on the 6th note of the Major scale.

184. ARPEGGIOS OF ii–V–I–IV IN MAJOR AND ii–V–I IN THE RELATIVE MINOR

185. IMPROVISATION WORKOUT – Scales over ii–V–I–IV in Major

186. MAJOR SCALE OVER THE ENTIRE ii–V–I–IV IN MAJOR

LESSON #14 *Scale Bracketing*

All Lesson #14 exercises are played with Straight 8ths.

187. DORIAN MODE AND MAJOR SCALE OVER ii–V–I–IV

188. MINOR SCALE AND HARMONIC MINOR SCALE OVER ii–V–I

189. IMPROVISATION WORKOUT

190. COMPARE THE MINOR SCALE AND THE HARMONIC MINOR SCALE

191. HARMONIC MINOR (starting on the 5th) AND MINOR SCALE OVER ii–V–I IN MINOR

PERFORMANCE SPOTLIGHT *Ipanema Dreamin'*

Ipanema is a famous beach in Rio de Janeiro, Brazil. The **Bossa Nova** is a type of Latin music which originated in Brazil and became very popular worldwide in the 1950s and 1960s. Antonio Carlos Jobim's "Girl From Ipanema" was a big pop hit for Stan Getz (tenor sax). In 1965 it won a *Grammy* for "Record of the Year". It is one of the three most often recorded songs in history. Notable musicians associated with the Bossa Nova:

Antonio Carlos Jobim	Astrud Gilberto	Joao Gilberto	Sergio Mendez
Edu Lobo	Luiz Bonfá	Roberto Menescal	Hermeto Pascoal

192. MELODY WORKOUT

193. "IPANEMA DREAMIN'" – Full Band Arrangement

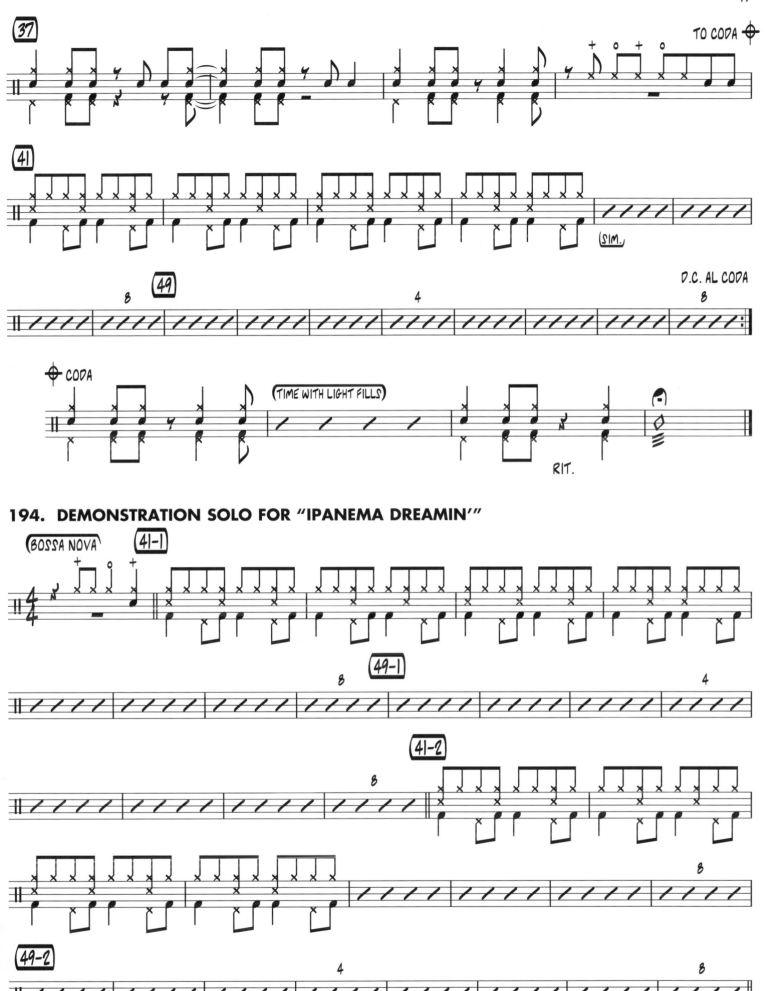

194. DEMONSTRATION SOLO FOR "IPANEMA DREAMIN'"

195. PRACTICE TRACK FOR "IPANEMA DREAMIN'" – mm. 41-56 (4 choruses)

PERFORMANCE SPOTLIGHT *Skating In The Park*

The **Modern Jazz Quartet** was one of the most successful small ensembles in the "modern jazz era." **Skating In Central Park** by pianist John Lewis is one of their most famous compositions. "Skating In The Park" is a tribute to that song and to New York City, the home of Central Park. New York City became the most important center for jazz music in the last half of the 20th century. Nearly all the great jazz musicians in history have performed at New York's most famous jazz clubs: The Village Vanguard, The Blue Note, the Savoy Ballroom, the Village Gate, the Five Spot, and Birdland.

Theory Concept – *Jazz played in swing style in 3/4 time can have a variety of accents.*

196. RHYTHM WORKOUT

197. THEORY WORKOUT – Chord Vamp I and ii in Concert E♭

198. IMPROVISATION WORKOUT – Major Scale over I and ii Vamp

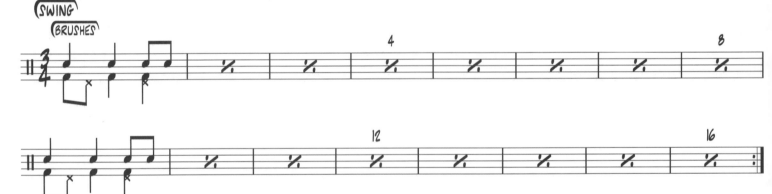

199. MELODY WORKOUT

200. "SKATING IN THE PARK" – Full Band Arrangement

201. DEMONSTRATION SOLO FOR "SKATING IN THE PARK"

202. PRACTICE TRACK FOR "SKATING IN THE PARK" – mm. 41-48 (6 choruses)

PERFORMANCE SPOTLIGHT *Five's A Crowd*

West Coast Jazz (often referred to as "Cool Jazz") is a style of jazz music that developed in the 1950s. West Coast Jazz was more sedate than bebop or hard bop. One of the most important recordings in this style is Dave Brubeck's *Time Out* which experimented with various time signatures. The most famous song from *Time Out* was "Take Five" by saxophonist Paul Desmond, which used the time signature of 5/4. Desmond was Brubeck's musical partner for many years. Important musicians associated with Cool Jazz or West Coast Jazz include:

Miles Davis	Gerry Mulligan	Dave Brubeck	Chet Baker	Lee Konitz
George Shearing	Shorty Rogers	Shelly Manne	Bud Shank	Art Farmer

203. RHYTHM WORKOUT

204. THEORY WORKOUT – Two Chord Vamp in Dorian   *Listen, then play. Pick any note.*

205. IMPROVISATION WORKOUT #1 – Using the Dorian Mode Over the Two Chord Vamp

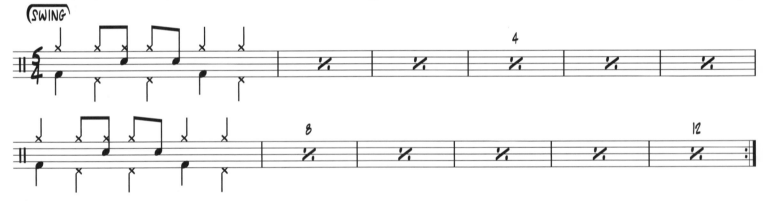

206. IMPROVISATION WORKOUT #2 – Chord Tones

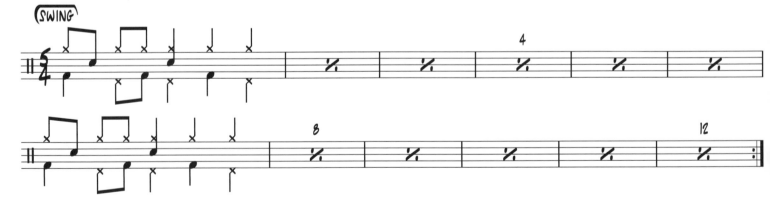

207. MELODY WORKOUT

208. "FIVE'S A CROWD" – Full Band Arrangement

209. DEMONSTRATION SOLO FOR "FIVE'S A CROWD"

210. PRACTICE TRACK FOR "FIVE'S A CROWD" – mm. 25-32 (8 choruses)